# Table for One, Please

Eleni Sophia

Eleni Sophia – Table for One, Please

Copyright © 2023 Eleni Sophia

'Table for One, Please'

All rights reserved.

ISBN: 978-1-914275-57-9

Perspective Press Global Ltd

# DEDICATION

I dedicate this book to the wonderful soul who has chosen to embark upon their journey of self-love.
The one who decided it was finally time to choose herself first. The one ready to take on the world with a new and evolved mindset.

'Table for One, please' are very powerful phrases – your ability to sit at the table alone and not care about the opinions of others whilst being present and mindful in your own world is a powerful tool many aspire to have but is mastered by very little. By the end of the book, I hope you find the courage to say these powerful phrases without fearing the opinions of others. I pray you find the motivation and courage through these words to do something different and take yourself out of your comfort zone.

Your self-love journey won't be the easiest but it will be a journey of discovery. Self-discovery is one of the best tools one can acquire in this lifetime; knowing who you are at your core will shape almost every experience you encounter. Once you find that love within you'll never feel so empty again. I promise; you will fill that void on your own

The journey of self-love is ongoing; that's the best part; once you begin, there is no going back; you are on this forever journey to get to know who you truly are. Once you're committed to yourself, that's it. And that's also why you shouldn't be so disheartened if you're going through a rough period; please, let it hurt, but also, let it heal. Give it the chance to work for your betterment.

It is up to you to take care of yourself, it's your responsibility to make sure you have you. And you will reach this stage – it will take its time but be easy on yourself.

Learning to forgive yourself for things that didn't go so well in your life and learning to comprehend that everything that didn't go so well in your life happened *for* you is one of the best decisions you can make - but this only comes once you begin nourishing yourself.

Self-compassion and grace are vital ingredients in this journey. Whenever I used to hear 'We are spiritual beings having a human experience' I would become very emotional. Think about it. Think of how rare it is for you to exist – yet your creator knew how powerful you were and brought you into this beautiful world – he'll never allow you to experience anything he doesn't think you can't handle.

You will come back to your better self. I pray you find joy in your self-love journey.

Thank you for following me on this journey. *Good Morning to Goodnight* was purely about heartbreak - a place for you guys to find solace. *This One's for You* was for all you wonderful souls to find yourselves and become the incredible unstoppable souls you are. *From Ours to Yours* was written by myself and my soulmate; we came together to share our love for one another with the rest of the world; to teach you the power of bringing back old school love, the nonexistent honeymoon phase, and to love unconditionally. *Breaking the Cycle* was for all my generational curse breakers; to remind you to stay on your soul's calling no matter how difficult things may seem. This book, this one teaches you how to get to the stages where you are one and whole on your own first. Teaching you the power of your solitude and alignment in one's own company.

Don't be fooled by this title – I am a firm believer in the divine feminine – the feminine that allows herself to be taken care of, the one who understands the importance of radiating her feminine grace, the one who understands the divine masculine is not bad – she understands not all men are the same - she's willing to give love another chance but she just needs herself first; she has nothing but love in her heart. But, for her to attract the divine masculine, she must be whole and complete and allow God to lead the way first. 'Table for One, please' is about cherishing the times you have alone – learning to embrace the beauty in your solitude.

The first chapter talks about some fundamental laws of the universe and is your reminder that everything will be okay. We all had this information before we set forth into this world; we knew we were always being taken care of so use the first chapter as a refresher. I know when we're in a place of hurting it is often hard to understand that things are working in our favor but I urge you to read this book with an open mind.

The second chapter is one of my favorites; you are the only person who can save yourself, Yes, you can read books like this that provide comfort for a while but they will only work if you're willing to do the inner work and healing. 'Saved by Her Faith' is the epitome of reading books like this and actually writing over the margins and understanding the power of your faith.

'Table for One, please' demonstrates the epitome of this cycle; from a place of hurt to a place of love, fulfillment, and awareness of one's self-worth. This cycle won't happen overnight – it'll probably take months but understanding your worth and what you bring to the table will make you limitless. The months of hard work will be worth every minute you spent working on yourself.

The most beautiful part of starting a self-love journey is that it never ends. The moment you decide to choose yourself, you will always choose yourself. You will constantly be wanting to improve your life. That's why starting the journey holds so much significance; it's a never-ending journey of taking time for yourself and always putting yourself first. Now that you've experienced this heartache, you know who you never want to be again and by prioritizing your self-care you'll never allow yourself to reach that level of hurt again.

If your purpose is to be a mother or a wife, you will be learning to love yourself wholeheartedly and you'll slowly begin possessing the qualities of a mother and wife; your cup will be so full you can begin pouring.

The sooner you let go, the faster you begin your self-improvement process. I wish you all the love in the world as you embark on this journey.

Life and its universal laws

Saved by her Faith

Table for One, Please

You won't come back to yourself;
you'll find your better self
and realize how powerful you always were

Life itself is a journey – we always have that one heartbreak that changes us for the better – the universe has an interesting way of shaping our path. Heartbreaks are funny because they can arrive in any form – whether it's in the form of a romantic heartbreak, not receiving a job you wanted, or even if your life changes in a way you never imagined. They find themselves to us in the most mysterious of ways.

Now how we heal from these and how we come out of these periods depends on our perspective. We can sit and dwell on why these things are happening to us or we can use them to shape our lives for the better.

Most purpose is found in times of disappointment; it's almost as though the universe gives us these opportunities to rejuvenate and cleanse ourselves from old habits and people that are no longer meant for us. If you're experiencing hurt, see this as an opportunity for nourishment. When you find yourself crying, tell yourself this is your body cleansing itself from all the pain and making room for new blessings to find you.

Your ability to use this energy as a fuel for motivation to become not only a better version of yourself but to use this pain to create will be one of the best things you will do.

As a beautiful and fresh year approaches us, many of us have set ourselves goals and resolutions - please remember to be kind to yourself whilst attaining these. As humans, it is in our nature to become worked up and so focused that we forget to cherish ourselves and give ourselves extra doses of self-love - aka human fuel - the most fundamental ingredient in helping us grow and achieve our potential. If you have set yourself certain goals and you forget one day, start over. Yes, each year is a wonderful opportunity to restart with a blank page but so is every day, hour, and second. With each breath, you are blessed with growth opportunities. Once you begin viewing each breath as an opportunity, you realize there is so much strength in the ability to start over. We did not come forth to earth as perfect beings; we came as the perfect creators; we can manifest and create change at any given moment. Take advantage and be grateful for that. Look at how much we have experienced in the past two years; individually and collectively, we have grown and evolved so much; I'm sure there were moments when some of us didn't even think we would make it this far. And look at us now. Be proud of yourself and, most importantly, remember that each day is an opportunity to love yourself more.

In a world that's always on the move, it's easy to get caught up in the chaos and lose sight of what truly matters. Take a deep breath and slow down. Cherish the little things and find joy in the simple pleasures of life. Your unique flaws and imperfections are what make you beautiful, so embrace them with pride. And remember, time is a precious commodity that can never be regained, so spend it with those who fill your heart with love and happiness.

Life is a precious gift, and every moment is a new opportunity to grow, learn, and explore. Embrace every experience, both good and bad, for they all have the power to shape and transform you. Accept the present moment and trust that everything is happening for a reason. Time is a finite resource, so choose wisely who you spend it with. Surround yourself with those who bring out the best in you, who lift you and help you shine

You don't need the answers all the time. As humans, we want to know 'why' but sometimes that why isn't in our control and we simply must trust that this was just how life was meant to play out. You entered this world, a unique being with a soul's calling. You have a purpose, a life mission. Whether that mission in life is to simply be your true authentic self, whilst making the world a better place, whether it's becoming a parent, whether it is building a corporation that helps millions, or even if it's just to enjoy your time here and simply just *be*, you have a purpose attached to your soul. And every experience you face in life is shaping you and helping you to find your soul's calling.

This life, this world, this universe is endlessly magnificent and as you begin to realize the potential you hold within this miraculous space, you understand the beauty of this earth and it all becomes clear; there are no losses in life only lessons.

Now I understand if you're experiencing hardship all this might be difficult to hear – so it's important to take each day at a time and wallow and heal before you accept this mere fact that the world is working in your favor. You have made it through every difficult situation you thought you would never conquer, and the universe will never put you through anything it doesn't think you can handle. Your creator chose you to go through that hardship because it knew you were strong enough to conquer through. Once you accept that every circumstance is here to help you grow, you view life from a completely different perspective.

You may not be happy with where you are in this moment in life, but this is not your destiny; you have the power to change the circumstances in your life; your creator hears every one of your prayers; he may not answer directly, but through symbols, people, and opportunities, he will always answer. You have only lived such a tiny proportion of your life – you have the power to create a wonderful future for yourself; just make sure you make the next years the best you could have ever imagined. I pray you find the courage to view life with this perspective.

You are one with the universe; it is completely okay if you are yet to find your purpose or your soul's calling; for it shall come to you in divine timing. You are a powerful being with infinite potential.
Let your soul guide you.
Remember to trust your intuition.
I hope these words give you the comfort you deserve; whether you take my words as motherly love or advice from an old friend, you are welcome back here anytime to make yourself at home. Whenever you need these encouraging words to find yourself and your power, come back here. Make yourself at home. Write your story. Most importantly, remember, you are exactly where you are supposed to be.
You are boundless, limitless and your potential is endless. Greatness, abundance, and happiness are your birthright. The moment you took your first breath you sealed your contract with the universe, and you knew everything was rigged to be in your favor. Use this book as a tool to design your affirmations. Allow your subconscious to receive.

Your greatest chaos, - bringing the most peace — please have faith that it will. I know things may seem tough right now but the ability to trust and follow your intuition whilst trying to take as much care of yourself is important in breaking free. Listen to the steps your heart is telling you; when you ask the universe for guidance and clarity, it always responds. Begin to be aware of all around you, the highest power speaks to us through symbols and occurrences in our lives. It is listening to you - it feels your urgency, it knows your desires

When you sit in prayer and ask your creator to heal your heart, do you think he's not listening? He always hears you

Sometimes impatience is the root cause of our downfall. We want something so much; we ask the universe but it doesn't deliver. We become frustrated. This is where faith comes in. The moment you affirm everything that is meant for you will make its way to you and if it's not, it shall pass swiftly. You train your mind to believe it so. It's one thing to affirm, it's another to believe. And that's where the importance of affirmation and repetition comes into play. By repeating wonderful affirmations, you train your mind into believing it's already true. Your mind doesn't understand the difference between now and the future. Whatever you desire is already yours. The universe has wonderful plans for you my darling, just show it a little bit of faith and watch it all fall into place

Sometimes it will test your patience but the moment you allow your creator to take over, he feels valued. He feels your trust. He will make this life a wonderful one for you - you just have to believe he will. Allow him to take care of the rest and just have faith he will. Watch how your life miraculously changes.

And as you sit and ask your creator for all that you desire and your heart is filled with nothing but pure intentions, I pray your prayers are fulfilled in the most divine timing of them all

God put this desire within you for a reason
It will find you
Everything you desire is making its way to you.
Align
In a galaxy so huge,
You are exactly where you are meant to be
The universe needs you
Your timeline has brought you to this very moment-
Inhale
Exhale

Your job on earth is to amplify all the beautiful things that make up your soul and to use them to serve others. You have talents, share them with the world. Through your grief, provide wisdom, through your sorrows, teach others joy.

Your path is unique; as long as it makes sense to you, that's the most important thing. If people don't understand your decisions or your relationship, it's not theirs to understand. It's yours. So, whatever you do, do it because you want to. Do not let others influence your journey or decisions

You have the entire world at your fingertips; you are an ounce of faith away from all that is meant to be yours.
Life is nothing but a game, the universe is your number one fan, your crowd, your team, and your instructor, it gives you everything you'll ever need, listen and grow.
It will show you, the moment you took your first breath, the world was rigged in your favor.
There is nothing in this world that you cannot be, do, or become.
Fix your mindset, become *you*

You are here for a reason; you are in this body for a reason. The body that houses your soul, the body whose cells heal themselves after getting hurt, you are magical- why do you question it so much?

We are all so magical, we are here for a reason. Throughout this book, I urge you to understand your journey on a deeper level and read this with an open mind. I believe we find everything for a reason, so whether you have picked up this book yourself or if you have been given this as a gift, please give a moment of appreciation that you can pick up this book and can read.

There is endless knowledge still unacknowledged by many beings - and everything we experience allows us to see things more clearly - there are signs everywhere - the universe speaks to you through these signs and that's why consciousness is vital - it allows us to see things more clearly. Everything around us is a blessing; we are always surrounded by blessings.

This world is so big and full of so many beautiful opportunities that once you start believing that everything is coming together for you, blessings will inevitably fall into place.
The beautiful journey of life starts from the simple act of faith and trust
Knowing and trusting that you will be okay
Knowing and trusting whether things are going the way you wish or differently,
In actuality, everything is coming together for you.
Life is so magical  And there are so many beautiful things awaiting you;
After every failure or lesson is derived an opportunity
Everything is a lesson- even sometimes when life feels like it is getting 'too much.' You are just evolving and growing
and most importantly in times like these, it's important to remember
You are never alone;
He's got you

Remain teachable; be a student in all aspects, every moment becomes an opportunity – one that helps you grow and evolve

There is so much healing needed in this world; especially internal healing. Why is it so difficult for humans to be happy for the success of others? We post photos of our food, and we receive hundreds of likes but the moment we announce a new business venture, we get half the amount of engagement. As discouraging as this may be, I invite you to understand this is a reflection of them and how they feel internally. It has nothing to do with your craft. You have to build such strong foundations within that you keep going; the lack of 'likes' on social media should not discourage you from achieving your best. There are very few souls who will be genuinely happy for you during this process and it's important to keep them close. Many people fear who you will become and it's important to not let this discourage you from achieving your potential.

Anyone who is doing better at you in life will never make derogatory comments about you or your plans. Whether that's doing 'better' through the form of happiness or accomplishments. Those doing wonderful things in this world simply elevate; they're so focused on improving themselves and helping others become better versions of themselves that no horrible words of discouragement could ever bring them down and stop them from achieving the success they deserve. If you're doing wonderful things - whether that's running a business, a charity or simply following a life that isn't considered the 'norm' and people are still trying to bring you down - I think we all know that means one thing. Nobody will watch your every move as much as those who have some element of envy within them. Those who are content and at peace with who they truly are within will never bring you down. And that's why security within oneself is important; once you build a solid foundation within yourself and you're satisfied with who you truly are, no words, no matter how harsh they might be, can bring you down. Train yourself to be happy for others; you pave the way for more blessings to enter your life.

Nobody should ever tell you you're speaking 'too highly' of yourself. You should be grateful you've reached a solid foundation of self-love to be able to respect yourself in this manner. If removing yourself from circumstances that no longer serve you is called 'childish' or 'selfish' then so be it. But if you're able to remove yourself from any table, circle, or circumstance that no longer serves your purpose - understand you have achieved a level of peace many in this life crave. This underlying foundation of self-respect is so fundamental - yes, losing friendships and relationships is upsetting so allow yourself to heal. But also, if you're aware you'll be the topic of the table as soon as you leave - do you really wish to surround yourself with such energy? And that's one of the reasons you need yourself first. Respect yourself first. Train yourself to deal with any negative situation and remove yourself with grace. As humans, our energy is sacred and as women, we already carry our future generations on an energetic level; it is our job to protect them. You must be so comfortable with sitting and owning the table alone first - be conscious of who you allow around you. You'll feel an exhilarating feeling of liberty - all negative ties will be removed, and you can continue flourishing and thriving without the negativity disrupting your peace.

We are all born with absolute faith
Oneness with the universe
The divine is always listening to you
But are you listening to the signs?
You possess everything you need – everything is within.
Your mind is your biggest asset, and you should treat it as one
All the tools, guidance, and clarity you need is all found within -
Listen.
**Take a deep breath and just *be***

Permit yourself to mess up; life is not a straight path. Do not entrap yourself; you must fail over and over just come back and respond with greatness; do not let your limitations restrict your greatness
By limitations I mean physical limitations; after all, we are endless spiritual beings with endless potential

You have time
You are exactly where you are meant to be
At this very moment,
you are in the right place
Anything that is not yours to carry, let it go.
Release. Exhale

When there is something on your heart and you know, you're destined for greatness
Take the action. You have absolutely nothing to lose
And it's okay if you haven't figured it all out yet.
Please do not let others' success and paths define yours
It doesn't matter if you don't want to follow societal expectations, you do not have to follow the rules your family or friends have set for you
This is your story – let's write a beautiful one

You are a powerful being
Your cells metabolizing,
Your body is the external shell protecting a soul that heals, that grows
Show it gratitude
cherish it by consuming your body with endless self-appreciation
Your first love should be yourself

Remove yourself from situations that no longer serve your purpose
Take a moment to think about this
We are on a sphere with a circumference of 25000 miles, orbiting around an even bigger ball of fire
As we surround ourselves emerge ourselves in nature, we realize how tiny we are
Your angels are protecting you
The universe is working in your favor
Just trust
Please
Trust
Have faith
divine timing
... awaits you

Do some soul searching; the only way you can find and create who you truly are is to go deep within; spending time alone, growing and evolving in different ways but most importantly become as uniquely you as possible

Remember that hardship you thought was the end of the world, you conquered it alone. You did that. Begin giving yourself the credit you deserve. May you continue to thrive

You have everything within you, the tools, the focus, the alignment, it's all there. Tune in and listen to your calling. Keep going sweetheart; you have no idea; you have the world at your fingertips

You are blessed in many ways; sometimes the simple understanding of this fact can be the best form of self-care; detaching from your current situation and sitting with a calm state of mind can be one of the best forms of self-love. Understanding your blessings - helps you appreciate all that you have and allows your creator to bless you with more. The simple art of understanding the beauty in all that you have
**is the most beautiful quality one can possess.**

The moment you adopt the mindset that everything is working in your favor; and that everything is happening for you, you liberate yourself in the most beautiful ways; even when the craziest thing happens, you take a step back, breathe and say 'its okay; this is happening for me; my creator has got me' you free yourself and ask the universe to take care of the rest. In moments where you find yourself in traffic and everyone around you is frustrated, that's their misalignment. You are aligned, a person drowned in faith, understanding the concept of divine timing. They know whatever is going on, is happening for them or acting as a shield of protection. And when you show your creator you trust in his timing; he will continue blessing you in the most random of ways – showing you synchronicities across all areas of life.

There is nothing he loves more than gratitude and there is nothing he appreciates more than a person of faith. And as you learn to become the embodiment of faith, he shines his light on you – you begin radiating love and endless glow.

The moment you begin to have that confidence in yourself, others will look at you the same; you lay the basic foundations of how others treat you, from how you hold yourself. As a Godly woman or a woman of faith, knowing your creator is by your side throughout it all should help you understand how highly you should be holding yourself, queen.

Healing is a journey and it's okay to take things slow and take care of yourself. You have learned from your past experiences and have grown stronger and more resilient because of them. This growth and self-love will help you navigate future relationships and approach them with a more positive and open mindset.

Remember that you are complete and whole within yourself, and no one else can define your worth or happiness. You have the power to create your own joy and fulfillment in life, and allowing yourself to experience love can be a beautiful part of that journey. Trust yourself, be kind to yourself, and don't be afraid to open your heart to the possibility of love once again.

So, continue doing what's best for your highest good and nourishes your soul; sweetheart, your soul deserves to be nourished.
We step foot into this world as a whole; we knew what we came here for, and we knew our missions in life; there were no insecurities; at our core, we are incredible beings, but we become conditioned by those things around us, and our conscious and higher self-become separated

The power of a conscious mind should never be underestimated; awareness is powerful in all its forms

This world is so extremely beautiful
think about how ginormous the galaxies are
the universe knew how much potential you had to come
forth and live your purpose
it was aware of all the wonderful things you were meant
to do – even before you set foot on this earth it knew
It knew how much potential you had
So why do you underestimate your potential?

Just because you took longer than others, it doesn't mean you failed. Train yourself to be happy for others when they succeed or enter a new phase in their lives because ultimately, we are all on our own paths and we work at our own individual pace. Everything will come to us when we are ready; the universe likes to prepare us before it blesses us, always. And that might mean we may face hurdles along the way but that is absolutely fine because everything is happening FOR us NOT to us. Everything is also vital for our growth and that is beautiful. Once we let go and truly believe everything is working in our favor, the magical aspects of life begin to unravel and that is truly beautiful. Have faith, be happy for others, give gratitude, keep working towards your desires, and remember, it will happen in its own timing. Faith is everything

We are all here for our own unique purpose, so, whether a certain individual has done things before you or whether they are experiencing more than you are, it does not matter. Train yourself to be happy for others when they succeed because ultimately, we are all on our own paths, and we are working at our own pace. Once you have mastered this concept of being genuinely happy for others' success, not only will you notice how much you are at peace with yourself, but, the amount of faith you have developed in the universe will become evident. We have our own unique experiences and each path is different. So, if you want your dreams to come true, start focusing on yourself, start taking action, and plan your life- write down where you want to be in the next ten years, and sincerely believe that you are deserving of all the success that you desire. Your time is coming; one day you will have it all.

Your ability to shamelessly ask for all that you want will be a powerful tool – it amazes me how many people are missing out on endless blessings because they're just so afraid to ask. What is the worst that could happen in this situation? You'll receive a no? Sometimes we're so afraid of hearing 'no' and of rejection, we hold ourselves back from our own blessings. It's funny because I've genuinely believed everything in life is tied to the concept of faith. Even stepping out of your comfort zone, for you to ask, you must have the courage. And with courage comes faith. It's the beauty in all religions. The thread that ties them all together, is the power of faith.

Each week, I urge you to train yourself to just ask for something – you will be surprised at the number of people willing to give you what you desire. Just have faith that they will – and if some opportunities pass, it's important to understand other blessings are also on their way. Don't be so afraid to *just ask*.

Before we came forth into this world, we had complete awareness of who we were and the strength of our power; we sealed our contracts with the universe on how we would live our lives.

And we agreed. Knowing this should shield you with some comfort - everything you are experiencing, you agreed to, so you must know you will be okay. I promise, I know it's probably difficult to hear from a stranger but please take this advice as a mother's love - everything you are going through, all the hardships, all the beautiful things in life you experience, are helping you become a better version of yourself so eventually you, too can share your story and help people around the world

So, remember to give thanks to the universe for all the sequence of events in your life that have shaped you into the incredible person that you are today
An aura of white light protects you
The universe shields over you to guard you against all negativities in this world
You will find the power in trusting

I urge you to trust in this beautiful thing called life; often we're so consumed with external limiting beliefs, they become our own. Please remember, you set foot on this earth a uniquely whole and complete being, you knew who you were at your core.

I say in my book, 'Breaking the Cycle' 'the universe adores the ones who go against the norms because you define faith. You prove your faith. I'm not directly referring to religious or spiritual faith but the simple act of faith – just knowing that everything will be okay is enough for the stars to be guiding you along your way.' Be free; liberate yourself. You are on this planet for such a small period; enjoy yourself.
For your creator finds joy in your happiness.

With belief, we bloom

## Saved by her faith

This chapter is dedicated to anyone experiencing any sort of heartache and in search of clarity. I hope my words soothe any distressful emotion you may be experiencing, and I hope you understand that you will come back to your better self.

Often, when we come from a place of hurt, it's difficult to view life with clarity; sometimes, because of our pain, we make rash decisions. You are worth so much more than what this 'love' had to offer. I hope this chapter teaches you to slow down and be easy on yourself; I hope it gives you the power to view life more clearly; your time is coming.

When heartbreak finds us, we wonder what we did to deserve all the hurt that arrives with it, but we fail to recognize the beauty in the self-discovery process and how beautiful the outcome will be. After all, time and patience heal all wounds.

The moment you begin implementing these standards and foundations in your life, you lay the fundamentals of how others should treat you; the way you treat and respect yourself is the way others treat you.

Sometimes we lose ourselves in the process of loving another – we're so focused on everything we can give them, and sometimes we forget we need to love ourselves.

The very first heartbreak is the one that changes you; this is going to be one of the best things that happen to you. This heartbreak teaches you the importance of adding value to your own life – this heartbreak teaches you the importance of speaking to your inner child – the child who may not have necessarily received the love you deserved. During this period of inner transition, it's important to speak to your younger self and tell yourself that you've got you. Allow yourself to feel pain in this journey, you must experience these feelings to come out of this stronger

Being brave enough to feel hurt will help you come out of this stronger. I understand how it feels when you pour so much of yourself, you forget you needed love and affection too. This time is very important – it's vital in rejuvenating yourself and finally giving back to *you* – the one who deserves it the most.

And just when she thought she couldn't handle anymore, the universe put more on her plate. She was confused and hurt and she never thought she could handle all that pain. But the entire time, all these experiences and the pain were helping her evolve into the incredibly wise woman she was destined to be. The universe was training her to become the best version of herself. And so, one day, she decided to slowly pick up the pieces and began building her foundations for herself, by herself. She had no idea how thankful her future self was going to be; thankful she took this first step. She was ready to find her better self.

Often – especially as soft women – we want to nurture and give our all to another, but we don't realize the person who needs this the most is ourselves. The way you devoured this entity, why don't you start by speaking to yourself in this manner? Why don't you take yourself out on a meal? Why don't you begin putting this energy toward yourself? If this is difficult to do, see it as you giving endless love to your inner child. Often, it takes this type of heartbreak to teach us to put our needs first, we're taught to respect ourselves. And only when we reach this level of wholeness within ourselves, the universe sends us the right person who was always meant for us. This heartache is here to teach you. It is not here to put you through any pain; this pain is necessary, I promise. It makes you stronger, it helps you remain grounded and stay true to yourself.

I know it's difficult to comprehend – especially during times of hardships but you will come out of this a completely different person. You won't come back to yourself. You will come back to a better more evolved and refreshed being than ever. Whole and complete with or without another by her side. Why? Because if this process taught her anything, it's that her creator will always be here. No matter what she experiences.

If she can go through that much pain alone and come out as the powerful conqueror she is, she has absolutely nothing to fear.

And there will come a time when you will have to forgive without having received an apology
And it will be of the most difficult experiences
But once you let go
You will make room for beautiful experiences to enter your life
The moment you stop seeking external validation you realize you have everything within to become the person you were always destined to be
You were born with all the tools you need to create a wonderful life for yourself

Life is precious and you should be so proud of yourself for making it this far
The world needs you here
Please never forget how extraordinary you are

These moments of finding yourself won't happen all at once but day by day you will notice smaller improvements in yourself and your routine. The journey towards self-love is not the easiest but when you reach that initial state, there will be a moment of exhilaration where you are thankful for how far you have come will be. People often say after heartbreaks, you'll come back to yourself - but I disagree, you will always come back to your better self.
Once you're in that state of flow, you are ready to meet your new and improved self,
So, become excited to meet her - train yourself to partake in incredible activities, take yourself out of your comfort zone
She is going to be so proud of the woman you become

She fears nothing because she's aware of the presence of God
Everything she has; she has her creator to thank for.

She was there to help him achieve everything he put his mind to but in doing so, she lost herself. Little did she know what a blessing this was; she was about to find the best version of herself. A version she never even imagined. All that energy she was putting into this entity, the universe was going to shower her with self-love tenfold.

And not all days were the same, sometimes she would find herself in the happiest of moods, but a certain memory would pop into her mind making her reminisce all that they had. But this never stopped her; she still took each day as it came and decided to put herself first. The best decision she had ever made was choosing herself first.

*Spoiler alert*

You will become one of the best versions of yourself. This hurt is temporary, everything is temporary. Use this pain as an opportunity; you are such a precious gem in this world
This is your reassurance that you will be okay.
The moment you understand your value and power in all that you do, my goodness you will be so grateful for all that you went through.

You must take care of your health; the heart will always heal; but do not sacrifice other areas of your body for this duration. Mind, body, and soul, all require care, all require healing. Allow yourself to be sad. My darling I know this pain hurts so much but please take care of yourself, I know you probably have no appetite but start by taking small bites every small bite, know this is it, the start of your magical journey to become your magnificent self

My darling, your internal has been through so much; now it's time to heal, so treat your body as your temple, reenergize, and allow yourself to grow.

I want you to realize, just because you may have been treated negatively before, that does not mean love is bad. You may have a negative experience with love but love itself is beautiful.

Heartbreak is a process of healing; it doesn't necessarily have to be a negative occurrence. Your perspective is vital here, so I urge you, next time you're crying or you're in pain, to remind yourself, this is a process of healing. With every tear, you rejuvenate yourself, so you never allow yourself to feel this type of pain again. Immerse yourself in this experience for you will never be this person again. You are evolving, growing, and becoming a better version of yourself.

Right now, it probably doesn't feel like you'll ever be okay, but I want you to re-read this in a few months and witness how powerful you are, you went through that, and you found yourself. Unless you experience this, you won't know what you deserve. This is going to be one of the most exhilarating experiences of your life.

The healing process cannot be skipped; do not suppress your emotions, allow yourself to feel. I know right now, nothing seems worthwhile, everything seems worthless, but you must snap out of these thoughts. You are going to save yourself. You are the only one that can.

This process is about allowing yourself to feel grief and pain so you can fully comprehend who you are at your core and what you deserve.

Healing and moving on from what once caused you so much pain requires an incredible amount of patience, solitude, and self-love
But is a beautiful process;
it teaches you to deal with these things so you can focus on yourself and become better versions of ourselves
for ourselves

but by the end of it all
it will be worth every minute you spent alone; your creator allowed you to dive deep within and analyze what you want from this world
you searched deep within your soul
to discover the amazing opportunities this world has for you
now you know not to settle for anything less than what your creator has for you

If you're going through a heartbreak, I urge you to devote the next few months to yourself. We all have different approaches to healing, but the best way is to devote this time to yourself.

Sometimes we want to hurt the other person as revenge but memories, relationships, and friendships do not need to end in spite; the further away you stay from negative emotions toward the other, the better the outcome for you.

I want you to start putting yourself first
May your faith be stronger than your fears
Be the girl who started putting herself first
The one leveling up in all forms
The one grasping life with opportunities
Building, evolving, exploring, traveling
Even if it is alone

Now you need to save yourself. And the best way to save yourself is to devote this time and love to yourself.
Conserve your energy. Conserving your love will be one of the best things you can do at this time; we often want distractions we quickly jump to the next thing without truly healing ourselves. This approach might make it seem as though things are getting better, but the wound is only temporarily closed here, deeper healing work is required for you to elevate to the next level
Don't try and run away from them as the feelings will always resurface


Taking time for yourself closes wounds. The time taken for yourself helps you build solid foundations of self-love that you'll never be in a position to allow those wounds to open in the first place

You will learn how to rebuild yourself and cherish your own company. You might not know how to be alone right now so it's important to check in with yourself. Write a diary knowing one day you will re-read this as a better version of yourself, and write in the 'notes' on your phone. Find a cathartic space. Indulge in your space and silence, you are going to get through this, this pain you're feeling in your heart, you are not the only person going experiencing these emotions.

Slowly, months will pass, and you will find yourself saying, 'Table for one, please.'

If they can leave you and let you be, this is probably the best thing that can ever happen - this is not a sign of value. You deserve to be valued.

Oh, but sweetheart
embrace everything you experience
live
accept your situation
for time is so valuable and so precious
choose who to spend it with wisely

You are far from unlovable - the way you have been treated is not a reflection of you or your love, it is simply a reflection of who they are and their misalignment; it is not a valuation of the intensity of your love. Please do not spend this time questioning your flaws or what might be wrong with you; your flaws are what make you so imperfectly perfect. Eventually, they'll realize how special you were, and by then, you will have found your better self and won't accept anything less than what your heart truly deserves. They say if you can love the wrong one so much think of how much you will love the right one. But before you can love the right one, I urge you to take this time to find yourself. Understanding what you bring to the table is a valuable tool in building your future relationships; it builds the foundations of your self-love and eventually, the quality of friendships and relationships you manifest. It also dictates the level of respect you desire; how you hold and respect yourself is vital in how others treat you. The ability to go to a restaurant and request a 'table for one, please' and proudly sip your coffee with a book, knowing you own everything around you is important for this growth. You will be okay, and you will find yourself. And you will come back to yourself. You may not come back to your exact self, but you will come back to your better self and that's all that matters; you will have you again.

Take your time to find the best version of yourself; the time you invest in learning who you truly are will be rewarded to the best
Endless opportunities await your arrival
Times of hardship allow us to discover our true selves
In silence and stillness comes discovery
Do not underestimate the power of sitting alone
Embracing the hidden blessings in our solitude and silence is one of the best tools ever

She became guarded - it was difficult to break down the walls around her heart for it took years of work to trust one just to be shattered again
But all she needed was herself.

The walls built around her heart needed time to come down. It wouldn't happen all at once but knowing she had herself was all that she needed

It was going to take time to feel complete again. Complete within herself.
All she needed was time and presence with her creator

She built walls around her heart to protect herself from any potential pain. It was difficult to let people in now but she needed time. She needed to find herself again. She needed a reminder of her worth and only she could do this. This had to be done alone

vulnerable than ever
She needed time with her creator
Time in solitude
Time for him to remind her how amazing she was
Time for him to remind her she was created with his vision in mind
Time for her to realize she was created in the most wonderful image and with the most wonderful hands of them all
Time for her to find herself again
Time for her to be open to love again

She just needed time

The nights she felt the loneliest
the universe's protective light washed over her body, she knew she was safe; the moment she entered this world, she was safe.
Her faith saved her.
She was saved by her faith

And as you, too become aware of this protection, you dive into your state of flow
Each day you take yourself out of your comfort zone; give yourself the credit you deserve

And you will be tested along this journey but it is so important to stay true to yourself. And as temptations arise but you understand the power of stepping away and putting yourself first – you've won.

Time valued alone is precious – an opportunity to explore your innermost desires
so
Become present in your silence.
Become comfortable in your presence
The ability to enjoy one's own company is a luxury.
Finding value in time alone and not feeling lonely is powerful; liberty craved by many but mastered by very little

Finding inner peace in your solitude won't come easily but the moment you conquer sitting at the table alone you know you can achieve it all
As you rebuild each day, you will begin to learn what your soul actually craves. In solitude, we find inspiration.

Comfort in one's solitude is power
You will no longer tolerate the disrespect of others. You understand the power and peace that comes with one's own company.
Use these tools to build a wonderful life for yourself

Begin honoring yourself – appreciate everything you experience; we all dream of our prince charming. No more, dream bigger, fit your own glass slipper, you have the power to unlock your higher being, take it.

Be excited to meet the new version of yourself
That solid foundation of self-love is vital for growth and awareness of one's worth

The purest form of self-love is the art of trusting oneself. Trust your intuition for it is your creator and guardian angels speaking life into you.
You just have to listen

It's interesting how life works, most purpose is found in disappointment, agony, and some of the worst situations we can experience. Life is a beautiful thing; it works cyclically; I believe we came here so we can hurt, learn, and create; this inspires others
I know it's hard to hear
But take each day as it comes
I pray you are so fully healed
I can't wait to see you smile again
And be able to talk about your story without feeling any negative emotion
Then,
Then you will know you have healed
You will never allow yourself to feel this hurt again;
A new and evolved individual - no longer settling for less

The ability to grow and find your better self is often underestimated; now this won't be the easiest of journeys but the moment you take back your power by standing on your ground and conquering whatever they said you couldn't, the universe and your ancestors surround you in your presence and admire your strength and bravery.
That breakthrough that comes from heartbreak is one of the most powerful things that could happen to you. If you're brave enough to walk away from something that was never respectful to you or your being. Being able to walk away from that attachment is so powerful. The ability to wish people the best and walk away from circumstances that no longer serve your purpose is bravery at its finest And therefore, being complete and whole on your own holds so much importance.

There is nothing to gain from hurting the other person, let the universe take care of that. This is an opportunity for you to grow and evolve into the person the universe had destined for you. Personal growth is the best 'revenge'

And as she slowly picked up the broken pieces, she realized that anything was possible if she had herself, she had everything within to conquer
Endless opportunities awaited her arrival
And as she became present and realized all she needed was to reach a level of harmony within herself
Little did she know the universe was preparing her for all the wonderful things to come

This pain you are going through is temporary; please release your emotions, sit in your own space, and allow yourself to experience this healing process

Patience will take up an entire chapter of your healing journey.

And one day, when you use your story to help others and you talk about your experience with so much poise and clarity, it will hit you that you are healed.

## Eleni Sophia – Table for One, Please

A woman who is so rooted in her creator's words isn't afraid to conquer life alone; she's using this time wisely; her truth is woven into God's words; she's using this time to build her relationship with her creator and herself. She dines alone to understand who she is at her core; a Godly woman isn't phased by the opinions of those around her possibly judging her for eating alone – she loves it – she's devoted to cherishing herself so when its time to become a wife and mother, she's able to pour from a cup that is so full and she's able to take care of her home and her family in the most beautiful and protective ways.

Becoming a soft woman took rebuilding, it took sacrifice. It took losing many people who didn't appreciate her. She's a soft woman because she trusts; she lives her life with ease, effortlessly radiating love and harmony – lighting up rooms wherever she goes.
She is submissive and also the homemaker, she understands the power her man brings to the house; she knows both roles are different the perfect balance within one beautiful being. Years of hard work and sacrifice allowed her to realize that there was not much in the exterior world that mattered. Everything that she strived for came from within.

She's mastered the art of blocking out the outside noise and continuing to strive for more - she's en route to getting exactly what she deserves, and she'll get there despite the hurdles along her way. People look at her in awe; surprised at how much greatness she can carry within her, she never disappoints.

And one morning she decided that it was time to leash back onto her power
So, she did
She took back her power
Her entire aura was consumed with endless elf-love
She lathered herself in the love she has always craved
And day by day
She became addicted to her own company and the sensation of time alone
She remembered she was the only person who could fill this void
External validation no longer pleased her
And she didn't take one look back
She embraced her past
More importantly, embraced her own power

One day, someone will be saying the following words about you; you are going to inspire many souls with your story; I know you are going to be okay:


A few months ago, this same girl was in a situation she thought was inescapable. She was drowning in her sorrow, her only hope was herself. She spoke to her creator and begged for help. Her creator listened but first, it was important for her to understand everything she went through was vital for her betterment. She didn't understand this at the time but now, now she's thriving with abundance,
Radiating from within her is a glow unseen
She went through so much pain just to come out of it just as stronger; she couldn't see it at the time but now, it makes more sense than it ever did.

Everything is energy so please be careful with who you give yourself; whether physically or mentally; we are all souls having a human experience. Your spirit desires the purest of energies

Most importantly, forgive yourself and if it's hard for you to do so, remember the girl you were 10 years ago - forgive yourself for her; your inner child deserves the love and forgiveness the most. That child now would look up and see the woman you are becoming, so powerful, so vibrant, and she would feel nothing but pride knowing her future is secure

## *Table for one, please –*

One of the most powerful phrases you will find yourself saying upon your journey of self-discovery and once you become content with who you truly are. The ability to sit at the table alone and become truly harmonious in one's own company is beyond powerful;

Finding value in time alone
Finding comfort in your solitude
Is the most precious of them all

'Table for One, please' is cherishing your own company and owning it. It's embracing yourself and knowing you no longer seek external validation from the exterior world. When you know you can dine alone with happiness and grace, you and your faith are all you need.

During my journey of healing, I found myself saying these phrases so often and I felt more potent than ever;
the moment you're able to own the table and not worry about what others are thinking of you, you begin mastering the brave route to self-love.

Do not underestimate the power of solitude and comfortability in one's own company; many of us are afraid of sitting at the table alone fearing what others will think of us but, we're most likely encouraging others to do the same
Being able to own the table is an opportunity to connect with oneself – understanding your likes and dislikes – knowing yourself.

If you're single, take this as an opportunity to find yourself – spend time with your thoughts
Whether you're in a healthy relationship, the power of being alone should not be overlooked.
The Universe, God, your intuition, your guardian angels are all present and protecting you. So, whether you're at a table for one or with a loved one, be present.

'Table for one, please' isn't you being alone; it's knowing God is there with you; even though you're physically presented alone, you're fully aware of the presence of your creator. You understand at your core lays the entire universe. You find more value in your mindfulness and presence instead of encounters that no longer make you thrive and don't add to your value.

You'll realize how beautiful being in your own company is; understanding you don't need another to come and complete you. Coming to understand the true meaning of the saying 'self-love'. You get lost in your thought, you realize everything you want to achieve; you guide and inspire, showing others the true magic of self-belief and determination.

And it's okay if you've never known how much you're worth because this is a journey. Understanding your intrinsic value – who you are at your core is the most important thing.

No matter what value you think you have based on this dimension, you were made in the image of God. You were made from the most omnipotent entity and you're here questioning your worth?

It doesn't matter how much money you have, it doesn't matter what types of clothes you wear; none of these exterior factors contribute to who you are at your core. We are so much more than *this*! We are so much more than social media, we are so much more than this external world. Many of our souls have experienced different lifetimes and here we are questioning our worth due to external factors? No, my darling. Give yourself time to see who you truly are. Who your soul really is and all the beautiful qualities it possesses.

Value doesn't come from others, it comes from within. Take your time to sit at your 'table', realign, refuel, and then go and take on the world. Just as you push and will yourself on, know the universe is always watching over you.

For every step, you take alone, God walks with you. Be open to blessings; for there is inspiration everywhere. Connection is just as important as solitude, it's the importance of finding balance. Human connection is often underestimated; we're all connected - in more ways than we can imagine.

There are so many wonderful souls in this universe - each with an incredible story untold.

The power of reinventing yourself is so immense; whilst it may take a while to see the process, there are still background improvements happening each day. Reinventing yourself
Day by day she is becoming a high-value woman – she knows her worth and is no longer settling for less; she creates her own opportunities unafraid to voice her standards and what she wants from this world

Heartbreak does not define you; your experiences do not define you, your outlook on life and how you conquer everything is what defines you.

Oh, you thought your first love was special, just wait until you meet your new and evolved self. Your first love is what you think love should be – you're vulnerable and often naïve. Don't get me wrong, first loves are beautiful in the purest forms but the learning and growth process that comes from the first heartbreak is simply unimaginable

You meet what you deserve

She listens intently to her higher self for she knows she is being guided

and cares for herself

Her soul is made of stardust

She is the purest of them all

One of her best features is she will forever remain true to herself
Even if she has to stand alone, she'll never give up on what she truly believes in
And that makes her respectable; admirable,
unafraid to speak the truth – even if the entire table disagrees; she stands firmly on her ground;
She was made to be different

I know how tired you are. But once you realize you are the only person you have, and you have all the capabilities of loving yourself just as much as you crave from another. You will be completely, entirely, and exclusively unstoppable.

Impossible to forget
She lingers in your memory.
You wish you would have treated her better
But that's okay; she has herself now
She devoted time to herself- invested in herself
She's grown and evolved now
She knows what she deserved
So, believe me when I say she won't settle for anything less
It went from good morning to goodnight to thank you God for that awakening
I pray you wake up from this illusion and you realize how much you really deserve from this huge abundant world

## Eleni Sophia – Table for One, Please

She doesn't even ask for much
All she's ever wanted was time
She doesn't even ask for 24/7 — she just wants to be felt like a priority again
But she knows she must be her own hero
I mean, you must, right?
Everyone is busy but it's who you make time for: it's who you prioritize and makes feel important — boy, especially a woman like her — the one who would have been down for you, who would have stuck by you, who prioritized you —
She's busy too but she always makes time — and funny thing is, she's actually out in the big world but she still made time for you
Regardless, she knows
Whether she has a knight by her side or not
She will always conquer

Eleni Sophia – Table for One, Please

Nothing is wrong with you
Nothing is wrong with your love
Your love is not flawed
You were just with the wrong one
The one who couldn't see your worth
And that's not your fault
Stop blaming yourself
You are so incredibly worthy
The moment you notice how much you bring to the table
You become unstoppable
Always remember
Give yourself time
Time is such a beautiful concept
Take this time to find what you truly want from this world
Your next love should be yourself
The best of them all.

She wanted it to be her, but you failed to see her for the incredible woman that she is
But that's okay because her life was not meant to be spent with you
It was meant to be with someone who deserves her
Who treats her for the amazing woman she is
She had no bad intentions
Nothing but the purest intentions for you
But
She's moved on now – fulfilling all those dreams she told you about, the ones you were meant to conquer together –
She was going to do it all with or without someone by her side

Just because someone failed to see you for the incredible person you are it doesn't mean you don't carry the credentials and credibility of a wonderful human. Your kindness is still appreciated by many, your love, and your affection will be valued by someone who deserves you and I pray you don't lose sight of this.

...

Spending and devoting this time to yourself will be one of the most valuable decisions you make because when your true love does arrive, you will know how to love him. Why? Because you're now pouring from a cup that is full of endless self-love. Remember in the first chapter where I mentioned once you begin your self-love journey, there's no going back – you're going to be so complete and whole as an individual entity, wanting to devote your life to another – and you're going to be vibrating in the most wonderful frequency that you would have manifested someone who loves and treats you exactly the way you deserve.

Never dim your glow for those who do not see your vision
You are on your personal path and
There is inspiration everywhere
Self-love is not only about loving yourself
True self-love is loving yourself enough so you can love another
Self-love sets the foundation –
The manner in how you view yourself
In her loss she found clarity
She remembers, in every situation is derived a blessing
There is gratitude to be found everywhere
With a soul emitting nothing but compassion, love, and strength;
she is not perfect but her liveliness and
More than half of her beauty is found in her mind
She's strong, composed, and ready to take on the world

You were made to be someone's wife
But first
You were made to love yourself;
You were made to encapsulate yourself with endless self-love
I have always known I was made to be someone's wife
Ever since I was young, I saw myself
It was never the 'huge wedding'
It was always dreaming of the person and the way we'd live our lives together
In our own little home
And as our family grew so would our home

## Eleni Sophia – Table for One, Please

Many people have little faith in her
Many people wish to see her fail
But she would never let that interfere with her hustle
She hustles harder than anyone you know
And she carries the purest heart-
She loves seeing others succeed-
Whilst striving for it all.
She's a firm believer in divine timing.
To some, she's crazy
To others, she's 'too ambitious'
But believe her when she says
She will accomplish it all.
Some days she falls
But she's strong; her experiences shape her
She can pick herself up
With or without support
She'll continue to accomplish and achieve it all
Because she's *her*
And that's her superpower
She's the hardest worker you'll ever meet
And she loves to see others succeed
she's striving for it all
to some, she's crazy,
to others, she's 'too ambitious'
but believe her when she says
she will accomplish it all

To the amazing, intelligent young woman reading this,
Keep working towards your goals,
Keep striving for what you deserve,
Keep working hard & continue lathering yourself in self-love & self-care
Keep your head high
May your faith forever be strong —
Keep investing in yourself.
For you are your best asset
Always

Put yourself first beautiful girl
Start that thing you have always dreamt of
Who cares if it's already been done?
You are you and that's what makes you so incredibly different and powerful
Launch that lipstick brand
Launch your podcast
Stop waiting for Monday or the 1st or for the New Year
Take this time to believe in yourself and to build your faith;
With faith,
We excel

There is something about her
There's an endless amount of brilliance radiating from within her
Her heart is beautiful
But my goodness, her mind
You will be blown away by her thoughts and integrity
Her beauty will always be a bonus,
But external beauty fades
Her mind is full of knowledge and wisdom to share with you
People are ignited by her energy
Drawn to the wisdom and intelligence she has to share with the world
You only encounter a woman like her once
You will consider yourself blessed to have even met a goddess like her

**Finding oneself**

The once-in-a-lifetime love you crave
You'll only get when you understand who you truly are;
Before you choose anybody
Make sure you have yourself first
Self-love is the foundation of everything that enters your life
A journey of self-love begins with *knowing*. Knowing you are deserving of all the wonderful things in the world.

Taking this time to become in tune with your higher self and learning what's best for your highest good is going to be one of the best decisions you will make

Recently, I became so overwhelmed with social media, I lost myself for a period and I felt so low. My constant posts had no meaning behind them; they were just *there*. I knew that for the sake of my greatest good, I had to remove myself and stop being so focused on others' opinions of me. The way I carry myself and the way I feel about myself is the only thing that matters – my happiness, my health, and my well-being. I had to do it for her.

She is art
Sometimes a little complex to study
An entire galaxy in her mind
Nonetheless, forever a wonderful luxury and asset to have

She helps you see life differently – a woman of faith here to make life easier for you; she eases the things in life, she contributes to others' success and doesn't see them as competition; instead, she sees them as sources of inspiration

And this entire time
And all along
All I had to do was put myself first
That's what I was being tested on, learning to be comfortable alone first
For the way you present yourself, the way you feel about yourself,
Draws a foundation for
That was the secret
Her art was her sanctity
When she needed to get away from the cruel world, she turned to art, not knowing the masterpieces she created would become the very voice the world silenced
No more empty promises

## Eleni Sophia – Table for One, Please

Nothing but putting yourself first from now own
She is in the in-between of happy, hurting, and healing
And should be so proud of herself for taking the first steps
You may have had a rough period and that's okay;
It's from these experiences that we learn to grow
And growth is everything
As hard as it is
She will take each day as it comes and whilst it may be one of the toughest things she's handled
She will still conquer
Cherish yourself enough to walk away/step away from those who do not serve you
And in the infinite of it all,
Through the art of helping others
She healed herself

Whatever you experience is lining you up for something so much bigger than this; you can handle this that's why you are experiencing what you are. Use this energy as fuel to help you find your better self. You will be so grateful that you utilized this time and experience and used it to your advantage

Learning to be your own best friend will take you places you've never been before. In your lowest moment in life, you often find yourself comforting yourself and speaking to yourself as though you would your best friend or even your own child. This is the love you crave and often, all self-taught coming from an abundance within. That best friend, big sister, or mother coming from within will start to guide you and clarify all your decisions. Your crying, is a sign of healing, as you rejuvenate into your new and evolved self

The frequency with which she lives her life is different now; she's composed, content, and thriving;

But when that love, you have always craved arrives, you will feel so liberated. As a result of this pain, you most likely will question everything; including its arrival but you must remind yourself that you manifested this love into your life. You did the hard work – you completed your inner work to be vibrating at the same frequency as this love. You deserve this.

Life is so beautiful; I've always had this knowing that all will be well. I was just born with this knowledge. Often, it takes heartbreaking experiences to understand the true beauty life holds. This true knowledge of being free and at one with the universe

You will randomly find yourself smiling, becoming more gracious as that soul within goes from craving love to creating it

Remember, the moment you can speak about your story with so much poise and clarity, you know you are healing. It is in your birthright to have all that you have ever desired; I don't just mean material things - but the happiness, the home, the family, the love - everything you have ever wanted, you can have only when you realize you are deserving. Before these find you, it's important to build deep levels of self-love and appreciation for oneself first; gratitude is the secret to living a fulfilled life - it's the gateway to receiving; the ability to vibrate at the highest frequency opens doors for more blessings to pave the way.

But you must build these levels of self-love within yourself first; to be able to vibrate in alignment with this frequency.

Understanding what you bring to the table is vital in manifesting the type of love you have always desired; the ability to provide and take care of yourself before love has entered your life is a beautiful thing; I don't just mean material things; the ability to love and respect yourself before another has entered your life is vital in having these things yourself will be the best safety and security you will ever have.
Knowledge of this power and faith can take you places you have never been before

If she can heal herself through that much pain and hurt believe her potential
She will always conquer
She radiates at the highest frequency because she knows she's deserving of it all; the universe is her provider; he will always take care of her

I want you to
take a moment to appreciate the incredible woman you have become;
you've come so far;
you've learned lessons along the way
you've conquered hurdles you never imagined
You did that
Start giving yourself the credit you deserve.

One day may you look back and understand everything your creator put you through was just training you to become the person you are going to be

And with enduring faith, liberate yourself

Thank you, universe, for making me the way I am, for making me the conserved incredible woman I am. For making me the purest woman so I can be the most amazing mother and support my babies and watch them become the incredible souls they were meant to be. For helping me nurture myself so I can devote myself to you and my husband. For making me the high-vibrational woman that I am. Thank you.

Let gratitude for all that you have consume your soul

you must now put yourself in uncomfortable situations
for growth only arrives out of our comfort zone
Just like the moon, stars, galaxies, and their stardust
you are made from magic
and you will conquer it all


what you have in the end will be so priceless
unconditional self-love
ad awareness of your self-worth
happier than ever
all these things you are facing
are actually all the ingredients one needs for growth

Become your own always

you can't break a woman like that
no matter how much hurt she experiences, she's going to use every experience as an opportunity
am ethereal being, strong-willed, yet so delicate only a select few will ever know,
how much this woman exudes her amazing energy in everything she touches

and in the infinite of it all,
she healed herself

You have time beautiful girl – so why do you keep putting so much pressure on yourself?

Self-love is your ability to take criticism – it's your ability to walk out the front door bare-faced without the worry of what others will think
Finding this level of contentment will take its time – maybe months or even a few years – but once you devote this time to choosing yourself

Begin choosing yourself
Becoming imperfectly perfect…

You are a masterpiece, my dear. Every curve, every line, every scar and blemish tells a story of your journey. Every inch is a piece of perfection, so precious, all your quirks, even your flaws, all make up you beautiful. Just learn to embrace your individuality

She lives a soft life now; the hardships she experienced made her softer, kinder, and kinder to herself and others. after seeing her growth through this pain, she's open to experiences, she understands pain is important for power

But it's remaining a lady during the process – having your own values and cultivating the life of the Proverbs 31 woman – something I describe more in my book, 'Breaking the Cycle.'

Her soul has always been filled with adventure – the thought of travel, exploration, and knowledge was forever on her mind. Each new horizon broadens the mind and broadens perspective. All the adventures she takes in her stride knowing that her time was coming

And even when the love she had always craved from another arrived, she continued to pamper herself.

She caters to herself so she has enough to give to the one who deserves it the most

## Eleni Sophia – Table for One, Please

She was an explorer, an adventurer, a dreamer, and a doer
She knew she was protected in all that she did

Sometimes when life got tough, there was a voice in her head that told her things would get better and all that she was experiencing now was to encourage her growth and for her betterment.

All this hurt was minor but she had to take advantage of this time; times when she was lonely
At times when she felt all alone, she knew she wasn't actually alone; *He* was there; guiding her along the way.

All the times she spent alone, she was practicing mindfulness, her creator was training her to be present
She knew her time was coming
Her time to explore, her time to flourish was coming
Time for her soul to flourish -

She was ready to flourish now.

I once had someone tell me I was a 'loner' and whilst it was said as an insult, I took it as a compliment. This is my biggest flex – the fact I can sit at a table alone, the fact I can take myself shopping or on a coffee date, the fact I can treat myself, and sit down in my own solitude without the need for external validation is one the most powerful things one can possess.

But this doesn't come easy, it won't come all at once. I understand when you're in your lowest moment, you'll often wonder 'How can I reach this stage?' I can't exactly tell you how but day by day you'll come to find yourself again. Why don't you start by taking yourself to a coffee shop and re-reading this book? Write your own notes around the margins and make yourself at home; this is your safe space.

Please remember nobody can interfere with the blessings God has in store for you. Everything your creator has given you, he's given you because you are deserving. Most importantly, he knew you knew you were deserving; you were vibrating at the highest frequency of self-love & awareness when you aligned with these things and he knew you were ready to receive. Now, sometimes exterior energies may overstep their bounds and be disrespectful. But during these moments it's vital to stay true to yourself and understand how deserving you are; you have everything you have because you deserve it. You manifested that wonderful job, that opportunity, that incredible relationship. The universe saw how wonderful souls were as individuals and decided to unite you together. You deserve this kind of love. One can only truly flourish when they are happy within themselves and for the success of others. If they still have difficulty finding peace when seeing others happy, that's on them. Not you. What is meant for you shall never pass. Nobody can take away God's blessings for you - no human, no entity, no bad intent. Yes, energy is real but so is awareness. And with awareness comes power. With power comes faith. With faith comes God. Nobody can take away God's blessings for you…God's plans for you never involved others' opinions of you. She attracts all the beautiful things in life

You must allow yourself to be loved; you may have had a negative experience in the past, but things are different now. Look at you; embracing your flaws; you understand they make you imperfectly perfect. You cherish yourself differently now; you're happier in your own skin. Do not allow your perspectives on love to change because of one bad experience. If this second love isn't the one, don't be so afraid; you have yourself now. The journey of healing won't be so lonely. Your outlook on life has changed and you're your own best friend. You are entirely complete and whole within yourself no matter who comes and goes, you're perfectly fine. You must allow yourself to experience love. Things are different now. You have yourself.

## Also by Eleni Sophia

**'This One's for You'** a poetry collection about the power of self-love and finding oneself.

**'From Ours to Yours'** a collection written by Eleni Sophia & pn.writes – where the couple discuss the nonexistent honeymoon phase, interfaith, and the power of appreciation

**'Perspective by Sophia'**- a motivational book, where Sophia simplifies the 'law of attraction' and encourages you on living a life that you love, just by changing your mindsets!

**'Good Morning to Goodnight'** the rawest collection about 'love' and first heartbreak.

**'Breaking the Cycle'** a collection of the power of breaking generational cycles, embracing your femininity and the beauty in balancing a career and motherhood.

She's the type of woman you know is going to have it all. Just one look at her and you know. Not because other people believe in her, but because she believes in herself. She's the one breaking all the generational curses; she's known as the 'rule breaker and the troublemaker.' And she's okay with that. The outside noise is just noise. We often hear, 'Tradition is nothing but advice from the dead' and my goodness, how true is that?! She's forever the protector of her future home, partner, and children. And as she becomes aligned and in tune with her higher self, she embodies her truth. Clothed in self-love, filled with ambition, and protected. You'll fall in love with her magic. She knows she will have it all.
**– Breaking the Cycle by Eleni Sophia**

Wish them the very best  And let them walk away  If they don't want to be a part of your life anymore  Maybe it's time for this particular journey to end. And I know it's hard  It is so incredibly hard; You're left wondering what you did wrong  But I urge you to shift your perspective; If you can give so much compassion to the wrong one  Think about how much you will be able to give to the one meant for you. The fact that you were able to show so much emotion shows how much you can love, and that is truly magnificent.
Maybe one day you will cross paths grown  and evolved
You will look back with clarity  And realize why things happened
If they are meant to be in your life  Inevitably,   It will happen.
For now, Continue to put yourself first  It's finally time to start making yourself a priority  Putting your happiness first. You deserve everything this world has to offer and more  Learn to give it to yourself first
You will see why.
**– This One's for You by Eleni Sophia**

**About the Publisher:**

Perspective Press Global is an independent publishing firm representing authors under the age of 20.

At Perspective Press Global, our mission is to inspire young aspiring authors that there is no such thing as being 'too young;' your voices deserve to be heard.

The firm was founded based on Sophia's struggle to find representation when she was a 13-year-old writer.
We now have published young talent from around the globe – including, the UK, Albania, Kosovo, Ireland, and Australia!

If you're interested in joining our team, please visit our submissions page at perspectivepressglobal.com and come say hello over on Instagram @PerspectivePressGlobal

Signed copies of all books can be found on perspectivepressglobal.com

For Eleni Sophia's work follow @EleniiSophia

Copyright © 2023 Eleni Sophia

'Table for One, Please'

All rights reserved.

ISBN: 978-1-914275-57-9

Perspective Press Global Ltd

www.ingramcontent.com/pod-product-compliance
Lightning Source LLC
Chambersburg PA
CBHW030304100526
44590CB00012B/516